WORDS I WISH TO HEAR

Poems & Epigrams

Pratham Dixit

Words I Wish To Hear

"to those who feel unheard,
and to those who seek solace in words,

this book is dedicated to you
may these verses bring comfort and joy
and remind you that you are never alone.."

Words I Wish To Hear

I have written many poems over the years

but you're the only one that I could ever live

Love? It whispers

He wasn't looking for the moon or the sun to
be in her heart

just enough light to pull him out of darkness

Words I Wish To Hear

My mother showed me that a person can love
you a million times more than they say

"I love you"

My father showed me that a person can love
you in a million ways without even saying

"I love you"

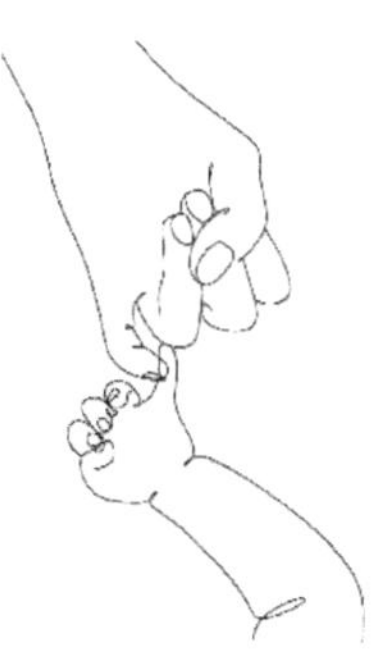

Maybe someday in the future

you will meet someone who is as messy as you

broken and chaotic

a little afraid of love

but always ready for an adventure

Whoever she loved she loved with whole
heart
Whoever she hugged she hugged with both
arms

I was darkness, she was light
to let her in was never a question or a choice

She wore the moonlight like a sweater
making the moon itself, smile back at her

She is pretty and complicated
She isn't calm but she is caring
She isn't dominant but she is daring
She keeps pain in her heart but spreads peace
with her smile
She is quiet at times but her company is
worthwhile.
She lacks motivation for herself but never
fails to appreciate her friends.
She knows what love is but somehow still falls
for what isn't.
To call her complicated is a beautiful
compliment
To call her pretty - a terrible understatement.

Words I Wish To Hear

dark skies
pleasant surprise
love stories
sweet memories
pain in disguise
and some hard goodbyes
each one of them
hidden in her light brown eyes.

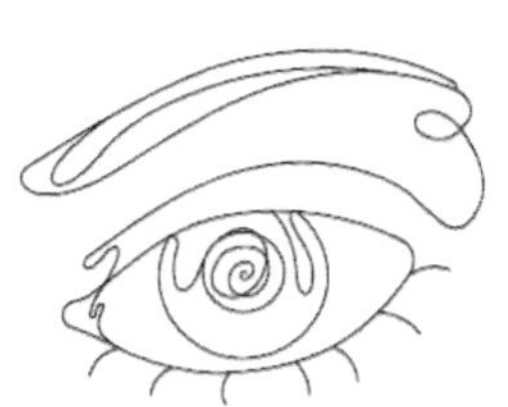

the human in her being is full of magic to be seen

He wanted her to be naked
naked at all the places
she was never loved.

He wanted her to be touched.
Touched at all the places
the fingers couldn't fetch.

Her heart was a broken land, no light , no
water, full of coarse dirt.

That's exactly where he wanted his garden to
grow.

Sometimes she is water

softly making her way through the tiniest of
spaces

and when she is not water she is fire

burning up everything in her proximity

She is not here to look pretty and settle in someone else's house like a painting on the wall. She is here to discover herself in all the different places she would go and wouldn't mind collecting a few scars on her way.

I want to go on an adventure with you
To all the places you're afraid of to go
I'll look for the ones that are somewhere in
you
and sow some seeds for the flowers to grow.

What a beautiful piece of art you are.
Made with both dark & light vibrant colours
of
joy & sadness
thrill & fear
peace & chaos
loneliness & excitement.
Pity to those who don't admire you long
enough
to notice the details hidden beyond their eyes.

You, my love, are what the stars look for when they look down

Damn those eyes

gives me warmth like sun

melts my heart like ice

There is no sun,
there is no rain,
it's a night without moon
and yet they bloom.
I know some flowers,
through the darkness they grow
when I saw you I knew
that sunflower is you

You are not an angel baby

they don't exist in real world

you are just a human being

but as good as a human can be

Got a heart so pure that everybody is scared to love

Perhaps loving me is like sowing seed in
graveyard your tree might grow with time but
will forever be alone at night

She is an open book written in a language the world hasn't discovered yet

*Her love for darkness makes the devil a little
bit nervous around her*

and when it's all sad & gloomy
and you find yourself alone,
you'll have me tip toeing into your heart
ready to sing a song that makes
both of us dance along

Silence shared with the right person

has pretty much everything that

needs to be said

Words I Wish To Hear

You're someone worth looking at all night
someone worth fighting for all life

You're not someone to be a set reminder for
You're someone who never slips off the mind

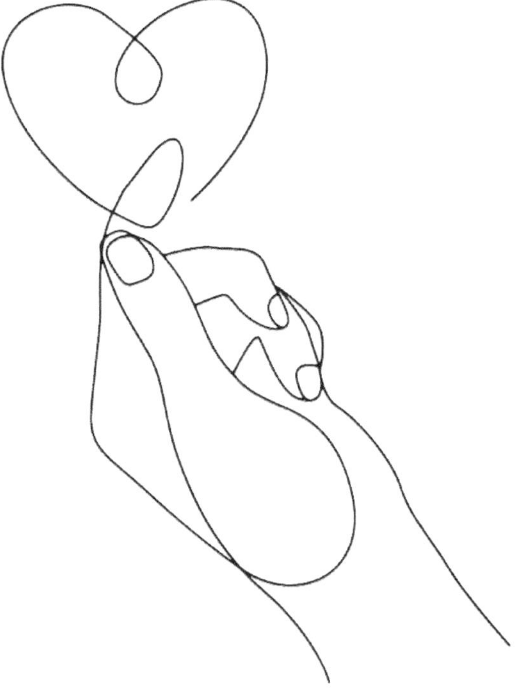

Words I Wish To Hear

If you take me back to the first time when I
was with you in the middle of the night and
you tell me there are going to be a countless
number of nights when I'll be without you I'd
still kiss you the same.

You'd ask me, "why?" and I'd tell you "you
won't get it cause if you did I wouldn't have to
face these nights alone".

You'd then leave, thinking why I wouldn't kiss
you more unaware of the fact that I never
kissed you less

I need a hug but not just any hug. I need a magic hug. A hug that pulls me out of my corners and brings me together. A hug that is warm enough to melt my insecurities and tight enough to not let me fall apart further. A hug that is long, long enough to fix me. I need a hug that is a shelter a hug that is a safe place like home. I need a hug that's wild to my demons but soft to the skin. I need a hug that holds my breath and instils life in it. A hug that goes in like a medicine and heals where it hurts. I need a hug that wraps me like a cocoon until my wings are ready to fly again. I know I am asking too much in a hug but I don't need just any hug,

I need a hug that is yours.

"It's a bad idea to fall in love with me", she
said.

"Bad idea, of course!", he said, "I love bad
ideas."

He wasn't satisfied while he went on to explore her body, her sweet spots were a pure bliss to kiss, which he did, but he wanted more. So he went in further, searching for her scars, her cuts, her wounds. He wanted to kiss them all. Everything that her body offered he was there to kiss and everything she was scared to offer, he kissed them even more.

Let's hold each other's hand and
move like the clouds in the sky
not knowing where we would go
and where we would end up
but as long as we are moving
we will be a beautiful sight to
watch

I wish I could kiss you
I wish I could say this to you

She was a different kind of lover
the one you'd find
sitting in a subway alone
listening to songs and
keeping her phone
close to her heart
or the one you'd find
sitting at the terrace
looking at the stars and
talking to the moon
or the one you'd find
lying on her bed with a laptop
playfully swinging her legs
while scrolling pictures of him

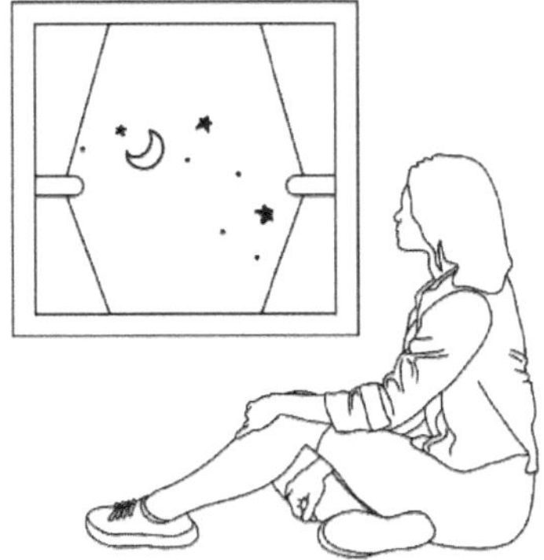

To the stars that listens closely

when she sits in conversation with
the moon,

wish I could pluck you from the sky

and put you down in these pages

To be in her proximity
is to live in peace amidst calamity

Her hair swirled like light summer
breeze
Her presence making trees breathe
with ease
When she walks out carrying her
confidence and charm
It's the nature who fights with time
just to have a glance

She reads a book like she reads a soul
turns the pages like she's touching the skin
feels the words like they're the heartbeat
and lets the story take her in

and when the moon fails to show up for the
stars
she is there sitting under the sky sharing stories
about her scars

Feelings that can't be expressed through mouth are felt through eyes

I like how the sea comes in

to kiss the shore

more than a thousand times a day

while the sand just sits there

unbothered about it.

It's pretty much how I've loved

in my entire life

reaching out of my depth for people

who wouldn't move an inch for me

I like the scent of your skin
smells like a thousand stars
that I could never taste

Love at least has given me stories to tell and poems to write

My love for you is like a flame,

burning strong without a name.

But as an introvert,

it's hard to show,

and sometimes I fear you'll never ever know

Being shy & quiet, I often feel like my emotions aren't quite real but they are there and they are true, even if they don't always show to you.

Her wildness is her beauty

Her freedom is her strength

Love her for who she is
not what you want her to be

She is made of bewilder
thoughts and wild dreams

Books aren't enough,
need to read your eyes
to find stories
these authors failed to write

Pratham Dixit

In the depth of her soul a
million oceans have drowned

She smiles at strangers and laughs
                    at every little thing
and he loves her for that

Some people are magic while

some are tragic but

she in all fairness is the best of both

The human in her being is
full of magic to be seen

Pratham Dixit

The best parts of your life are small and tiny,
always hard to notice.
hiding in corners,
too shy to come out
unless you hold their hands
and ask them to.

Kindness is not weakness
but a strength that comes from within
it takes courage to choose love
when hate seems like the easier win.

You are too good to be someone's once upon a time

You are a paradise

a bag full of everything nice

Words I Wish To Hear

I feel the energy more than I hear the words

I don't stay because the words are sweet

I stay when the energy is real

Fall in love with the idea,
the idea of building a beautiful life together
but do not fall in love with the promise
because promises can be broken.

Fall in love with the actions that

witnesses a commitment to the idea

the consistency in showing up every day,

the effort put into making it a reality

and the willingness to work through it all

together and forever.

Go out in the sun
let it shine on you
It's cold out there
let it take some warmth from you

 between coffee and sleep, I'll always
choose you.

THE FIRST HUG IS THE STRONGEST DRUG

I carry her in my heart

in my words

and in my art

Sitting at the terrace gazing at the stars

every thought of you was a healing to my
scars

75

I couldn't find a place for myself in her world
hence I created a place for her in my words

He wrote about all that he loved

and no one ever asked him

why he never wrote enough about himself

Heartbreak? It Echoes

To be a writer is to be vulnerable

to cut yourself open to a world that only
knows how to hide

Words I Wish To Hear

Broken crayons still colour

Broken hearts still love

But you can't expect a blue crayon to colour
red

or a broken heart to keep you warm

Some of us don't want to put off the fire
burning around us

because it's the only warmth we feel, once in a
while

Words I Wish To Hear

I just want to be alright
Step out of the dark and see the light
Whatever it is I wanna fight
Figure out what's wrong, what's right
When I'm alone, I wanna hug me tight
Perhaps, find the courage to share my night
If I end this right now, it'd be just fine
But I want to live this life, even if it doesn't
rhyme....

It's the silence of this empty heart

that troubles me more than

the loudness of my chaotic mind

Words I Wish To Hear

No don't look at me like I matter
I've been fooled before by eyes
that gave me hope only to leave
me in shatters

"Do whatever you want to do with me", she
said

"but don't look at me with any bit of love

 in your eyes that you cannot give"

I used to think there's nothing more liberating than having someone who loves you back the way you do but here I am feeling comfort in abandonment and freedom in solace

Few nights are quiet and then comes the
tsunami

you thought you were finally moving and now
suddenly you are drowning

Words I Wish To Hear

These nights, they hold me
and sometimes I hold them.

We both understand each other
We both know how it feels to be empty and
alone
Always there but so hard to notice.
These nights, they don't scare me
cause I've been with them for so long.

I've seen through them, I've seen how scared
they are of themselves and they've seen me
through.

These nights, they know me so well.
They know I don't talk much, they know I'm
so tired to speak up,

so we both share this silence now.

No crying no screaming.
Just us, quietly holding each other one by one.

When I'm asleep, these nights hold me.
When I'm awake, I hold these nights up

Between these four walls of my room
I feel trapped.
It's draining and it's exhausting
There's this window that I never open
because it's glass is weakened, by my constant
cries
Then there is this door, always open but still
locked
I have this table that offers me all types of
books
but never a tiny bit of concentration
My almirah, full of stuffs that I'm afraid to
touch again
and finally my bed, as untidy & miserable as I
am, all day
Everyone thinks I'm safe in my room
while I'm choking for life in here
I've forgotten how to fly, how to walk
cause in here I only crawl
I need no walls I need no shelter
save me some rain, I'm ready to face the
storm
Get me out, I'm not safe in here
before I close the door and my life

Words I Wish To Hear

You said you have a cold heart

is that why you burnt mine

to keep yours warm

He didn't fall for you he just tripped

and you see

that's where you got tricked

Words I Wish To Hear

Sometimes the demons inside are easier to
confide
than the people we meet outside
The demons may be scary,
but at least they're always there,

ready to listen and understand,
without judgment or demand.

It's not that I prefer demons over people,
but sometimes it feels like an equal
choice between two difficult options
and my friend you know already
which one of them offers a kinder reception

You ask me why I am sad but you're always in
a hurry
My sadness isn't one line caption, it's a whole
damn story

What do I do with your fingerprints on my
body that do not wash away?

What do I do when all I see are these
fingerprints and not myself when I stand in
front of the mirror?

Should I shed my skin to get them away or
should I paint myself with another body?

You ask me why do I hate them so much? I
tell you, I don't.

These imprints of your fingers etched all over
my body makes it more special and sacred
than any other but I ask you,

what good is a body to a man who has lost his
soul?

You took away all those beautiful mornings
when I opened eyes to see you

and left me all these dreadful nights when I
have to close my eyes to see you

Thinking of you helped me sleep tight, it's the same thought that now keeps me up all night

Soon the clock will hit 4am and I'll crumble again. With sadness pouring down on the bed I will look for sides to lay my head. With the corner calling me to sit and contemplate I'll get up wondering how I became a slave to my own thoughts. With my soul drenched in memories my eyes would see everything the darkness shows. With every part of my body crying to sleep I'll wait for the morning to hit my eyes and pull me out. When the light arrives I'll finally sleep, until it's dark again in my dreams

Some people are tapestry of scars

Some a mere collection of wounds

Pour my heart into your glass of
whiskey and it will work better than
ice

Words I Wish To Hear

THE SCARS YOU GIFTED ME BRING MY TATTOOS SHAME

Stay committed to your dreams

they are more loyal than human beings

Do not ask me to prove my love for you

I'm not here to be accepted, I'm here to be felt

Gift your absence to anyone who
doesn't value your presence

Words I Wish To Hear

"There lies the problem", she said

"you only listen you never observe
I tell you that I'm fine and you
believe that I am"

Sometimes I write

sometimes I bleed

sometimes I stich these words

so they don't scratch my heart

Somewhere in between your lies

you never noticed how my love for you died

Heart filled with dreams that didn't come true,

Head filled with thoughts that won't bid
adieu,

Feet moving forward, unsure where to go,

Carrying a soul heavy with burdens that
continue to grow

Just like everybody else, deep down I also want to feel loved and feel wanted.

I want to be desired and touched.

To be wrapped in the arms and feel the warmth.

I also want to receive those cute little texts and smile like a baby.

Go together on a drive to the hills then come back to sleep with a good night kiss.

I also want to feel the intimacy of two bodies and the affinity of two souls.

I want to feel everything that two person can possibly feel together.

But I DON'T KNOW WHY a hundred days like this feels better & safe than that one day of betrayal and withdrawal

It doesn't matter how good you were. It doesn't matter how much you did or how much you gave. It doesn't matter how many more miles you walked with your broken legs. It doesn't matter how many "I'm sorry" you accepted with a heart heavier than your own body. It doesn't matter that you spoke more with actions rather than words. It doesn't matter how many sleeps you skipped or how many hours you waited. It doesn't matter how many gut wrenching feelings you swallowed back instead of spilling out. It doesn't matter how many times you came back disappointed or how you let go of all the little things that ate big pieces of you. It doesn't matter how you managed to smile with a sinking heart. It doesn't matter how you stayed when things got tough and tried when nothing seemed to work. Sometimes doing more than everything doesn't matter. It doesn't matter if your flesh and soul took more than what they were built for.

Nothing matters,
except that you tried

and yes, that matters.

Pain made me what I am today. It may not have made me the most likeable and lovable person around but it did taught me why I shouldn't hurt people just because I am hurting.

> Pain taught me to not prick others with the thorns that I grew. It taught me to not bleed on others with the cuts that I carry. It taught me to not yell in someone's ear when I hear myself screaming in my head.
> No matter how bad the pain was, in the end it did make me humble.

I made my pain sit with me tonight.
I offered it a drink and I said
"If you wanna stay here, stay
you want my seat, you have it
you want companions,
you call hurt and misery
you do whatever you like to do in here
but if ever again you tried to take my place
there's only one way it's going to end for you -
painful.

I've been so ignorant lately

Walking past people
like they don't even know me

People are moments, they come and go
what stays are memories, and they kill you
slow

By the time we realise its real or
fake its already too late

My head aches trying to write things you
wanna read

My heart aches trying to write things I wanna
say

This struggle between mind and heart,

 leaves me torn and falling apart

When your heart catch feelings that your mind
refuses to believe and your mind tells you truth
that the heart refuses to accept, that is when
you look around for advice but find yourself
walking on a thin rope at this circus called life

It's a great challenge loving a broken heart
Perhaps a greater one when the heart is yours

I feel you everywhere except here

119

How far is too far?

Wherever you are

Sadness at times feels comfortable
to me.

A familiar friend that keeps me
company.

Though it may not be good for my
heart and soul,

this weight of sadness feels like
home

You didn't fight for me
You didn't fight for us
and now it has left me
at a place where I have
to fight myself for the
rest of my life.

LIFE IS A LESSON IT IS NO FAIRY
TALE

YOUR LOVE CAN BE REAL AND STILL
FAIL

123

It's been more than a year in your absence

and I haven't moved an inch or a half since

Words I Wish To Hear

Sometimes to write is to scratch your wounds

to dive deep into the pain that consumes you

to relive the memories that hurt you

and feel the emotions that never leave you

Sometimes to write is to bleed on paper

to face the demons that haunt you

to confront the fears that taunt you

but then sometimes that is what it takes

to write the stories that need to be told

for in these pages of brokenness

lies comfort to the hearts turned cold

To cry and sob is one thing and to absolutely break down in tears is another. People often break down when they're alone because it takes someone very special to let you be vulnerable and put your guard down and if someone has that person with them maybe they won't even reach that point, just maybe they won't. Come on, you only fall apart cause one - you couldn't hold yourself together and two - you didn't have someone who could've held you together. So just like that, I fell apart once I cried and I cried a lot but not alone, I did it in the arms of my person, the same hands that had hugged me for years, the same fingers that held mine for years. It was sudden. Like all bad things it came unexpectedly in a moment that was all smiles and joy. I cried, I shivered, I stopped and continued again. So what happened next? You would think that it's the perfect place and perfect time for one to take it all out, in front of someone who knows how to put you back together. Mind you, it was. In that very moment it felt the same, like all the weights were off the heart and it's a matter of time when you feel good again. What's strange was that I didn't knew what all that weight was about. I never cried like that before and now when I did, I didn't know why.

But the person who held me close to the chest knew everything. It's the same person who build up the tears was now wiping them off. I sat there having no idea about it. I didn't know it was the end, but the heart knows everything and I couldn't realize at that moment that my heart was crying out to a person who already had an escape plan ready for the exit. Yes, that person was prepared to leave and it's terrifying how I had my weakest self even before that person left. It's terrifying how a heart knew it would break but the person didn't

It's not about living anymore.

It's about getting through the day, day after
day

It's not about living anymore, it's about
fighting fights, one after another

It's not about living anymore, it's about sitting
in a corner and waiting for the night to pass.

It's not about living anymore; it's about
somehow leaving the bed pretending to be
fine

It's not about living anymore; it's about
wishing to be not here but anywhere

It's not about living anymore; it's about
avoiding your own self

It's not about living anymore,

it's about not getting tired of getting tired of
not living anymore

Do not waste your life waiting for something

that's never going to happen.

The hope that saves you sometime

is the same hope that kills you most of the
times

I   am   tired   of   their   games
they   put   my   heart   on   flames

I'm   tired   of   their   false   faith

Now I gotta keep the ashes safe

In solitude I find my peace, but sometimes it can be a painful tease.

For though I feel so much inside, my voice is often forced to hide

YOUR NO CAN BREAK A HEART

BREAK IT BUT NEVER SAY YES

WHERE YOU MEANT TO SAY NO

I hope you don't ever get to know what it's like to be lying on your bed at midnight and feeling like you are alone in the middle of an ocean, drowning, gasping for air, splashing your hands and legs desperately, trying to save your life.

what's poetry if it doesn't disturb you

what's truth if it doesn't haunt you

what's life if it doesn't scare you

and what's love if it doesn't hurt you?

Words I Wish To Hear

Ourselves? we discover

a little empathy to ask "what's hurting you, my friend?"
and a little courage to answer is all that we need.

I know that you don't feel like moving
forward.

You feel that you're stuck and you haven't
moved an inch from days or even months.

But listen, there's a tomorrow for you and a
day after it and then days after it so on one of
those days you will move.

I know you're sinking and the water is all over
your head but you're still breathing and as
long as you keep doing it, in all possibilities
you will move.

What you've lost is not always gone.

There remain the pieces and the more you look for them you'll discover how gently you've been home to the remains of all that you've lost.

Uncover your scars they are not a shame

they are your pride a sign that you survived

I hope the storm around you,
settles soon
and you sail through
to where the
sea meets the moon

You are the most beautiful thing about you, the way you look at yourself in the mirror and admire yourself for coming this far, the way you proudly say your name, the way you fill yourself up with the words you deserve to hear, the way you walk with pride of being who you are.

You are not perfect but look how perfectly you carry the imperfect you around.

/ / Breaking bones and aching heart
I wonder how she turns them into art. //

*She was fire burning brightly in
a world turned cold*

The biggest mistake she ever made was in
blindly believing that she wasn't worth saving

*I HAVE FALLEN IN LOVE WITH
THE TRUTH NOW AND TRUST
ME LIES DON'T BREAK ME
ANYMORE*

Either they'll realise your worth and
treat you better

or you will realise it for yourself and
walk away

The way I have lived my life it's almost a sin
for me to not be happy.

But to be sad is not a sin.

There is so much to feel in this world, so
many emotions yet all we chase is happiness.

It's normal to be sad for a while.

It's normal to be stressed over things.

It's normal to be not okay.

It's normal to not fake a smile.

It's normal to be worried and to cry when it
pains.

It's so normal to not be yourself at times.

What is not normal, I feel, is desperately
trying to be happy.

What if, on one of these nights, you quit?

"I'll be proud I didn't quit, the night before"

I noticed your smile
I noticed the pain behind
I looked straight into your eyes
I saw the darkness deep inside
I heard the beating of your heart
screaming how it was ripped apart
I felt the touch of your skin
hurting at places they committed their sin
I guessed your thoughts
how you wish you died
I gave you a hug
I know you still traumatized
I gave you my words

They became your voice
you gave me a promise
you made a brave choice
another shot at life
It'll be all peace, no strife

Words I Wish To Hear

The one to take care of you
The one to love you
The one to encourage you
The one to turn things around for you
The one to be kind to you
The one to tell you healing words
The one to share yourself with you is perhaps
you

Though you may never touch
the surface of the moon,
or travel to the galaxies that surround
your thoughts and actions ripple out
like waves across the space

You may not have the power
to change the course of stars,
but you can choose to shine brightly
in your own small corner of the world.

Though you may never carry yourself
beyond the boundaries of the universe
you can still roam around in
the magic of this verse

Words I Wish To Hear

Let me weave my words with care, for they
hold the power to inspire and repair.

To mend the broken hearts and soothe the
soul, to make the broken feel whole.

Let me craft each sentence with precision, to
evoke emotions and stir ambition.

To ignite the fire within and spark a change,
to help us all break free from the chains.

For words hold the magic to heal and unite,
to bring us together in times of plight.

So let me weave my words with care, and
spread hope and love everywhere.

Don't let the lines of a notebook trap you,

because people are too complex to be
contained in words

By being lost for a while, there's
a lot you can find

I find solace in the sky,

and comfort in the moon.

For in their vastness I see,

that there's a place for me

Words I Wish To Hear

I live in my own world loved and hated by my own self

When you chase something that
never wants to belong to you,
you end up losing more than you
can ever possibly catch.
For the things that truly matter,
they will come to you,
and those that don't,
you need to let go with trust

Words I Wish To Hear

The ones who burned all the bridges leading
to you
will one day cross oceans to come and see you

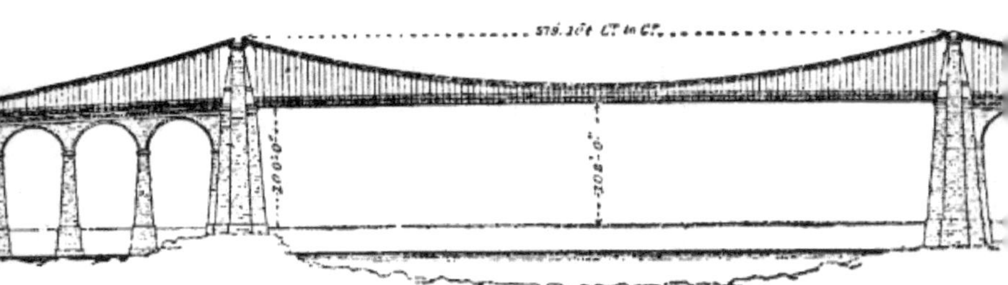

Every story begins somewhere and ends
somewhere.
You don't want to see the end and that is why
your story never begins

If you love the moon enough to keep it close
to your heart,

be brave enough to ride the tides that it
unfurls in your heart

Poetry for me,

is a bunch of stuffs that makes me smile

sometimes laugh and sometimes cry.

Sometimes poetry is trouble. It makes you forget about everything else, slowly pulling you closer to its little pieces that so badly crave to be put together.

It's pulls you so close to its intimacy that you forget about breathing unless you make love in between all the spaces of the words you wrote.

It keeps you busy until you've kissed each and every letter and lets you go only when you re-read it like a secret confession.

Sometimes poetry is trouble and when that poetry is a person, all you look for is trouble

Calm your head
soothe your soul
wash your eyes
moisturize your face
love your body
and never fucking doubt yourself again

Just like love healing will find
you and catch you when you
least expect it

On all my lonely nights
it was the moon that held me tight

To be broken is to be creative.

Just look at how artfully
you've pulled all your pieces together

Watch your words. Always. There's a thin line between saying what you feel and choosing the right words for the same. Cause when you speak you don't think about the other person, you don't think how they affect them, cause when you speak you have no idea what your words might make them do, what they might lead them to. So think about your words, cause when you speak you overestimate the other person to be strong, to be understanding, to be capable of taking it well but often it's not like that. I can write I can tell you this, teach you because I'm strong and very well capable of taking things as bad as they are but I know many of you aren't and many around us are not.

Many of us haven't been loved right, raised right, taught right and it's not our mistake when someone comes up to us and say things that absolutely shatters us and we feel like it's the end of the world.

 It's not our mistake but it's absolutely our mistake if we lead someone into this just because we couldn't watch our words.

t's okay to be out of sync with this world
to walk slowly while everybody's else is on the
rush

"you are not what you used to be", an old
friend said

"We are not supposed to be who we were", I
replied

"We can be a little better or much worse

but never the same person we used to be"

Words I Wish To Hear

Today I'm at peace

my body feels weak

but my soul is at ease

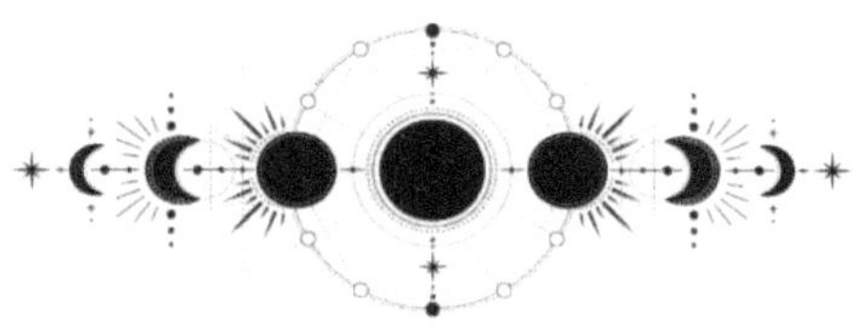

Half or full
The moon will always be enough

With or without you
I'll always be more than enough

Now I'm silent because I've spoken too much
to people who never listened

and with her own tears she
saved her burning heart

look at her now.
grown into everything
you never thought she'd be

YOU ARE A MIRACLE EVEN ON
DAYS YOU FEEL MISERABLE

Your worth is in your heart

so wear it on your sleeves

let them see what it is about you

that they can't afford to unsee

177

I treat my life as my home.

So if you're coming in,
leave your shoes at the door
and your ego on the floor.

Words I Wish To Hear

Rest, my dear head. take some rest
You've wandered to too many places
taking your caravan of thoughts
on your shoulders
you've visited too many past memories
like villages that now know no existence

Rest my dear heart take some rest
you've loved too many people who left you
for dead
you've felt too many feelings that remain
unsaid

Rest my dear soul, take some rest,
you've been searching for meaning, trying
your best
let go of the weight that's been holding you
down,
sit for a while and wear peace as your crown

Pratham Dixit

One day your chest wouldn't feel heavy like a
stone

One day your heart wouldn't be lying in the
valley of despair
One day your eyes wouldn't be watery like the
sea
One day your head wouldn't be filled with the
whines of waterfall
One day your legs wouldn't be fragile like
autumn leaves

Trust me one day your soul will feel alive like
a flying butterfly

I smile, I laugh, to hide the pain, but it never
truly goes away.

I'll keep on moving, day by day, hoping the
happiness will find its way.

For life's a journey, with ups and downs, and
sometimes the smile is just a frown but
through it all, I'll find my way,

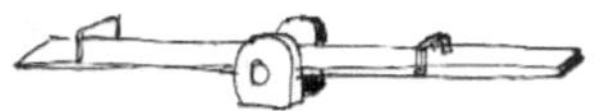

a bit happy and a lot sad, but stronger each
day

Poetry didn't come easy to me and I didn't let
it go when it was hard
Poetry didn't come easy to me and that is why
it stayed for long

I don't want a moved world, crossed oceans, climbed mountains or stars plucked out of the sky. They are big things for me and I'm not capable of keeping them. I want small things, imperfect ones, things that are different and uncommon. I want fallen leaves instead if a tree full of fruits. I want broken toys instead of soft stuffed ones. I want stained sheets, leaked pens, ripped pages and knotted threads. I want bruised skin, defeated soul, teary eyes and overwhelmed smile. I want rejected strangers, disappointed friends and heartbroken lover. I want poetries without rhyme, books without contents and novels without stories. I want every such thing that is not accepted and I want to accept everything that is not wanted.

*Sometimes it's the wrongly put
words that find the right places
in a heart*

Emotions run wild, like a raging sea,
each one unique, for you and me.
what we feel, no one else can know,
it's our own story, our very own show.

She clutched the letter in her hands, tears
streaming down her face.

The words written on the page were
everything she wished someone would say to
her.

But the words were written by her own hand,
a reminder that sometimes, the words we wish
to hear the most are the ones we need to say
to ourselves.

ACKNOWNELGMENTS

I would like to thank all my supporters for their encouragement and inspiration –

My Parents

My Friends

My Family Members

My Instagram Family

Canva for illustrations

And all my readers.

I would love to hear back from you

\ Visit me on Instagram at @typewriter.inks

Or

Write at depreciatedtypewriter@gmail.com

THANK YOU

XX

Pratham Dixit | Typewriter.inks

Words I Wish To Hear